For the Love of Gumbo, Let's Cook!

Creating Memories & Heirlooms in the Kitchen

To my dear Carolyn. Happy Cooking! Love GG

By Linda "GG" Gibson

ISBN 978-1-4507-3021-1

This book was written in loving memory of
my mother, Geraldine Stanton, and
my grandmother, Ella D. Smith.

Contents

Lost Bread, 117

Acknowledgements

I thank God, first, for the opportunities he has given me. I thank my children, my family, and my friends for all of their love and support. A special thanks to Cheryl Wilson, my friend and editor, without whom I could not have completed this book. My love and thanks goes out to all of my customers who have supported me over the years. This book would never have been possible without you.

Introduction...

Nowadays, the focus on family and friends is fading away, especially when it comes down to cooking a good 'ole homemade meal. Lots of folks don't cook anymore. Too many of us stop at the drive-thru or stick something in the microwave and eat in front of the television most nights. People think cooking is too much work. We're missing out on something special.

Yes, cooking is work, but it can be fun to work together. Spending time in the kitchen—and at the table—is how precious memories are made.

My fondest memories as a child came from watching my mother and grandmother cooking in the kitchen; the laughter, the rattling of pots and pans, the sounds of chopping vegetables; and then, the wonderful aroma of sizzling onions and garlic, sweeping through the house and causing so much anticipation. The anticipation of the meal was exciting! When the meal was ready for us, we were ready for the meal.

My mother and grandmother both shared what I refer to as "a black woman's blues". My mom was a single parent. My grandmother took up the slack to help her raise five children. They were natives of Natchez, Mississippi--the place where I was born.

In the early 1970's, my mother and grandmother moved us to New Orleans. As a single parent, my mother took odd jobs. Grandmother was a domestic; she cleaned houses and cooked for other families. I grew up on her Southern and Creole cooking--a delicious combination.

I like to say that I grew up in poverty, but ate in a five-star restaurant every night. Even though the menu could have been characterized as a poor man's meal, it was prepared, presented, and served as though it was going to a wealthy man's table.

Today, I am always asked the question, "Where did you go to culinary school?" And my answer is, "I didn't". I learned to cook from the skirt-tail of my grandmother. She was a self-taught master chef.

My grandmother didn't just make wonderful meals for wealthy families. She took what she learned, and incorporated it into a lifestyle for herself and her family. The dishes didn't match, but the food was good and the love was so strong, it made every meal worth waiting for. They taught us to bless the food first, and after we ate, we thanked the cooks. Then, a hug and kiss would usually follow.

Growing up in New Orleans was a wonderful cultural experience. It is a city with a soul for food. The flavors are like none other. Mix in African, Spanish, and French; stir it up, and Honey, you got Creole Cuisine! There is nothing like a good Gumbo. The spirit of New Orleans is IN the food, and once you've experienced it, eating takes on a whole new meaning.

I tried my hand at other businesses; but in 2000, after a family gathering, I realized just how much I enjoyed cooking, and watching my family and friends enjoy eating what I cooked. I opened GG's Coffee & Café in New Orleans in 2002, sharing family recipes from generations. The food was a hit. Soon, I was busy catering, serving lunch, managing a thriving business, and enjoying a lifestyle my grandmother could only have dreamed of.

Memories of food are so important. In the culture where I grew up, family fun, feasts, celebrations, fellowship, and sharing are all centered at the table. We never forget a good meal. It makes us humble, and it will put a smile on your face. Even in sad times, food brings people together.

On August 29, 2005, the tragedy of Hurricane Katrina destroyed my home and my café. I lost everything. Words cannot describe the sorrow and devastation of losing all of our material possessions and having to leave our beloved New Orleans. It was then I realized the importance of family.

My grandmother could not read or write, so I had
no recipes in her handwriting to lose. I lost many
other family heirlooms, including some of the pots
and pans she had passed on to me; but I realized that
the most precious things could not be washed away
by any storm: faith in God, memories, love—and the
sweet experience of cooking with my grandmother.

Almost a year later, I decided to finish the cookbook
I had started before Hurricane Katrina. It has taken
four more years to complete this book, while
working hard to rebuild a life for my family.
Through a lot of difficulty and by the Grace of God,
I've stayed true to my mission of spreading the joy of
food and family.

As we mark the fifth anniversary of Hurricane
Katrina, New Orleans is facing another tragedy
caused by the Deepwater Horizon oil spill in the Gulf
of Mexico. The oil tragedy seems nearly
insurmountable; but it's important to affirm the
resilience of New Orleans. My beloved city plays a
special role in our American culture, and New
Orleans is part of our National family.

Now more than ever, it is time to keep joy and
strength alive. We must support each other in every
way we can. At the table, we can hold one another in
happiness. Every time you cook, every time you sit
down to eat together, let it be a time of sharing and
happiness. We don't know what tomorrow will

bring, but we can make the most of today by remembering the simple pleasures of the table.

May the vibrant spirit of New Orleans live forever in our hearts and on our tables!

Linda "GG" Gibson
Woodstock, Georgia
August 20, 2010

How to Use this Book...

Now, this cookbook was written to be used. That means you should write in it!

Use the blank pages to include your own recipes and family pictures. Make plenty of notes. Feel free to add, subtract and substitute. Make it your own. This book is not just about me, it's about you, too! Use this book as a starting point, then fill in with your family's recipes and tips. Then, pass it on to your children and grandchildren.

I promise I will not ask you to fill your cabinets with spices that you'll use only once. I will not give you recipes that will take you all day and half the night to prepare. These are tried-and-true, easy-to-cook recipes that I hope will help bring your family back to the table!

I know everyone has a fond memory of a Mother, Father, Grandmother, Aunt, or someone in the family that created special meals. Take the time NOW to recall those memories and traditions---and, take time to share them with your family.

I hope my cookbook will help you create some traditions and memories of your own.

Happy Cooking!

Creating Generations of Recipes

List of Things You Will Need

First you need family and friends--then always keep salt, pepper, and onions on hand: honey, they're like the Holy Trinity of the kitchen! They can create instant flavors, but remember, always start out with a *little* salt and pepper.

You can always add salt and pepper to something, but you cannot subtract it. How do you know when the flavor is right? When it tastes good to you, it's right.

Simplify—it doesn't have to be complicated!

Always have a heavy pot, a heavy skillet, and a sifter on hand. There are a few essentials you should always have on hand too:

> Allspice (ground)
> Bay leaves (whole)
> Butter (NOT margarine)
> Corn meal
> Crushed red pepper pods
> Eggs
> Evaporated milk
> Flour (plain)
> Granulated garlic
> Granulated onion
> Gumbo file
> Nutmeg
> Salt, or Sea Salt is good, finely ground.

Baking Powder
Sugar
Pepper. Black or White, finely ground.
Powdered Cayenne

If you want other spices, feel free to add to the list; but, Darlin', I'm telling you, these really work for flavor.

Some Things You Need to Know

Everyone knows their own stove and oven. These appliances vary so cooking/baking temperature and time may need to be adjusted according to your stove top and oven.

When cooking, water can boil out causing food to stick so tilt the lid, do not cover completely.

Pasta and rice can overcook so don't leave pasta in water when done. Rinse and drain well.

When mixing cake batter, butter should be softened, not melted. Melted butter may make batter come out too soupy.

A pinch is almost a hint. A sprinkle can ruin the whole dish.

Darlin' Let's Cook!

GG's CREOLE CAFE

Bread

Bread doesn't have to be complicated, and it's just the right touch for so many meals. Find a place that sells fresh sandwich and French bread without additives and preservatives—stick with simple ingredients. Then, learn to make your own biscuits & cornbread—they don't call it quick bread for nothin'!

Auntie Janie's Cornbread

2 cups white cornmeal (plain)
¾ cup all purpose flour
1 teaspoon baking powder
(heaping)
1 level teaspoon salt
1 teaspoon sugar
2 eggs
3/4 cup buttermilk
1 teaspoon mayonnaise
1 cup whole milk (I call this
sweet milk.)
½ stick butter

Preheat the oven to 375
degrees. Place the butter into
a 10" iron skillet, and put it in
the oven, just long enough to
melt the butter. Remove from
oven and set aside.

◆ *An iron skillet is the secret to good cornbread. Season your skillet according to the manufacturers' directions*

◆ *If you have leftover cornbread, save a hunk for the squash casserole!*

Sift dry ingredients together into a bowl; add eggs
and buttermilk; mix. Add mayo and mix.
Start adding sweet milk, slowly blending it in.
Pour the melted butter from the skillet into the batter.
Stir to blend well. Spread the mixture into the hot
skillet. Bake in a 375 degree oven for 20 – 25
minutes or until golden brown.
To tell when the cornbread is done, stick a fork or a
toothpick in it and if it comes out clean it's done.

ॐ

I remember
my
grandmother
whipping up a
pone of
cornbread and
humming an
old Spiritual,
thanking the
Lord in her
soul for the
food that was
going on the
table.

ॐ

Garlic Bread

10-12 inch loaf of French bread
½ cup salted butter, softened
2 Tablespoons fresh parsley
½ teaspoon garlic salt
2 medium cloves garlic, minced

Cut the bread right down the middle.
Mix all other ingredients until smooth and creamy.
Spread mixture on both sides of bread.
Close together and wrap in foil.
Preheat oven to 375 degrees and bake for
approximately 15 minutes, or until golden brown.

Tip:

*If you want it to be
toasty, place bread
flat in a pan, right
side up until it's
golden brown.*

Grandmama's Biscuits

Remember to place the baking rack in the middle of the oven, because you don't want the biscuits to bake too fast.

2 cups unbleached all purpose flour
1 Tablespoon baking powder
¼ teaspoon baking soda
1 Tablespoon sugar
1 teaspoon salt
2 heaping Tablespoons shortening (room temperature)
2 Tablespoons butter (room temperature)
2/3 cup buttermilk
2 Tablespoons melted butter (coating)

Preheat oven to 450 degrees. Get your bowl for mixing. Put your flour, baking powder, baking soda, sugar and salt into the sifter then sift into the bowl. Add the 2 Tablespoons of butter and 1/3 cup shortening to the flour. Start cutting in your shortening and butter. To cut it in, use two knives to blend with the flour mixture, then break up the lumps with your fingers, until the mixture looks like little balls of dough. Use your hands, it's alright, they are your biscuits! Start adding buttermilk slowly with a spoon. You will see it forming into dough. Start working it. Knead just until it comes together. Don't over knead. If it seems a little sticky, dust with a little more flour. Roll out to a half inch thickness and cut with a biscuit cutter—or pull off a little dough, shape it and pat it. Toss biscuits very gently in the melted butter to coat. Place biscuits in a pan and bake for 12 to 14 minutes or until golden brown.

෨෨ঙ

I can see my
grandmother
standing there
with her
apron on. I
remember
these biscuits
for breakfast,
coming
straight out
the oven with
warm syrup
on the side.
Mm..mmm! It
brings me
back.

෨෨ঙ

Flap Jacks

Tip: Flap Jacks are thinner than pancakes.

1 Tablespoon sugar
1 teaspoon salt
1 Tablespoon baking powder
2 cups all purpose flour (plain)
2 eggs
½ teaspoon pure vanilla extract
½ cup buttermilk
2 Tablespoons melted butter
¼ cup water
You will need additional butter for frying flapjacks

Sift dry ingredients together into a mixing bowl. Beat eggs until smooth; stir in vanilla and add dry ingredients. Beat until smooth. Stir in buttermilk, melted butter and the water. Melt additional butter in a preheated skillet or griddle. Pour to the flap jack size you desire. Brown on one side then flip and brown the other side.

It's even better if the batter is made the day before. Great with grilled ham, bacon, smoked sausage, eggs, coffee or tea.

Serve with warm syrup. You can also sprinkle with cinnamon or powdered sugar.

Salad

Variety really is the spice of life, and salad adds variety to the meal. The freshness and texture of salad is a must for health and pleasure.

Simple Salad Sensation

1 head lettuce (iceberg or romaine)
2 tomatoes
1 dill pickle, sliced
Salt and pepper to taste
Mayonnaise as your dressing

Wash lettuce and drain really well. You can pat dry
with a few paper towels.
Slice tomatoes.
Add dill pickles.
Salt and pepper to taste.
Add mayo as your dressing.

My mom used to fix this salad all the time. She used
iceberg because she was a savvy shopper.

I love this salad with anything fried, especially
chicken and catfish, with a few French fries and
toast.

Mardi Gras Salad

Fresh mixed greens
Romaine lettuce
Cucumber, diced
Mandarin oranges or tangerines
Tomatoes, diced
Red onions, sliced
Granny Smith apple or
pear, diced
Walnuts (toasted)
Cheddar cheese
Mozzarella cheese
Croutons

Honey, this salad is a party in your mouth, AND it's good for you. Add turkey, ham, grilled chicken, grilled shrimp--it's so good.

Use as much or as little of each ingredient as you like.
Wash your greens, drain really well, and pat dry with paper towel.
To toast walnuts place on a cookie sheet in 375 degree oven for about 5-10 minutes, turning frequently.
Toss the salad and place in a pretty bowl; then sprinkle on cheese, add croutons and walnuts.
I recommend a sweet salad dressing, like honey mustard dressing mixed with vinaigrette.
Put dressing on the side and add as needed. Don't drown your salad, savor the flavor.

The Family Reunion
is in the Kitchen

Miss Sang's Fruit Salad

3 red apples cut in small chunks
½ cup raisins
½ teaspoon fresh lemon juice
1 celery stalk, diced
½ cup walnuts, toasted
½ teaspoon sugar
½ cup mandarin oranges
2 Tablespoons mayonnaise
¼ cup flaked coconut
Maraschino cherries, to decorate the top

Using a rubber spatula, gently mix apples, raisins, lemon juice, celery, walnuts, sugar, and mandarin oranges together. Stir in mayonnaise. Place in refrigerator for about 30 minutes.
Add coconut and mix. Just before you serve it, put cherries on top.

Great salad for a summer day.

GG's Chicken Salad Royale

4 bone-in chicken breasts
2 stalks of celery, chopped in pieces
1 onion cut in rings
4 cups of water
Salt and pepper to taste
Mayonnaise
2 teaspoon pickle relish (I like sweet relish.)
½ teaspoon GG's Bodacious Creole Seasoning®
4 croissants, toasted, right before you add chicken
salad

Wash chicken well.
Put chicken, celery, onions, and water in a large pot
and place on medium heat. Cook chicken until it is
falling off the bone. Drain all off the juice. Remove
all bones, and cut the cooked chicken into small
pieces. Add salt, pepper, mayonnaise, pickle relish,
Creole seasoning and mix. Add more mayonnaise if
desired, but not so much that it becomes soggy.

Great for brunch. Serve cold over a toasted croissant.

Cold Macaroni Salad

3 cups cooked elbow macaroni
1 cup med or large, frozen (cooked) peas
Salt and pepper to taste
Pinch of cayenne
¼ cup of sweet pickle relish
1 Tablespoon of Creole (brown) mustard
1/3 cup of mayonnaise; a little more for moister salad

Cook macaroni from package directions (until done.)
Drain and set aside.
In a mixing bowl, add other ingredients, add
macaroni and stir.
Refrigerate for about 2 hours.

Tip: Serve with ham
or turkey sandwich
and a pickle spear on
the side.

Spinach Salad

3 cups raw spinach
1/3 cup finely chopped purple onions
6 strips bacon, fried crispy
1/3 cup diced tomatoes
2 hard boiled eggs

Wash spinach and pat dry.
In a mixing bowl add all other ingredients except eggs. Toss.
Slice eggs for garnish. Use a salad dressing of your choice—I like Ranch or Balsamic Vinaigrette.

Broccoli Salad

1 bunch fresh broccoli
½ cup raisins
½ cup sunflower seeds
¼ medium purple onion, chopped
8 slices bacon, fried and crushed or bacon pieces

Dressing:

1 cup mayonnaise
2 Tablespoons wine vinegar, cider, or white vinegar
¼ cup sugar

Wash and cut broccoli into small bite-size pieces.
Mix with raisins, sunflower seeds, onion, and bacon.
Mix dressing and toss.
Refrigerate for one hour, then serve.

Salad Dressing

2 Tablespoons white wine vinegar
3 teaspoons fresh lemon juice (get the seeds out!)
2 teaspoons finely minced garlic
½ teaspoon of Creole (brown) or dry mustard
1 teaspoon minced fresh parsley
½ cup of olive oil
Salt and pepper to taste

In a mixing bowl, mix all the ingredients.
Let it set for a while, about an hour, then it's ready to serve.

This is great on any salad.

Soups, Stews & Sandwiches

Take it easy! These recipes make great weekday meals. Soups and stews freeze well, too.

Hearty Vegetable Soup

4 quarts water
2 cups onion, chopped
1 pound chicken drumettes
1 pound beef stew meat, boneless
1 medium potato, cut into medium chunks
1 can tomato paste
1 pound bag frozen mixed vegetables
1 cup canned whole kernel corn
8 ounce package regular spaghetti
Salt and pepper to taste

In a large pot, put 2 quarts of water.
Add a cup of onion and chicken drumettes.
Cook on medium heat until tender.

In another pot, add 2 quarts of water, 1 cup onion, beef and a little salt. Cook until very tender.

Tip: Spaghetti is tricky—it cooks fast--so when tender (al dente) turn pot off. You don't want to overcook your spaghetti.

Water tends to cook off, therefore watch your water and add more as needed. When beef is done, add beef, potatoes and tomato paste to chicken. Bring to boil, reduce heat to medium. Add vegetables, corn and dry spaghetti, breaking it into pieces. Add salt and pepper to taste. When spaghetti is done--about 10 minutes--the soup is ready.

Special Moments

About the Cover...

Family pictures are loaded with sentiment. Looking at those precious images takes you back to the past—an expression, a gesture, a story. The four pictures on this book's cover have a special meaning to me.

This is me, GG in high school, shortly before I married at 18 years old. I was the oldest of five kids; my mom had me at the age of 13, so I helped raise my brothers and sisters. By the time this picture was taken, it felt like I'd been grown up for a long time.

In this picture, I was about 4 years old. This is the only existing picture of me and my mother. When we evacuated our home prior to Hurricane Katrina, I took the picture off the wall, and placed it on top of an armoire in our house,

thinking that it would be safer there if the wind shook things off the walls.

We stayed with my aunt in Natchez, Mississippi to ride out the storm. Soon after the storm had passed, we were sitting on the couch watching the news coverage. At first, it looked like we'd been spared, and we'd be able to go home. Suddenly, they announced that the levies had been breached: New Orleans was under water. We were in shock. My first thought was that precious photograph. I got up from the couch and went to the back porch of my aunt's house. There, I cried and asked God to save the photo. Even if our house was ruined, I just wanted that one memento of my mom, who had passed away several years before.

After the flood waters receded and we were allowed back to our property, my husband and I entered the house. I screamed and cried as we waded through the mud that filled every room of our beautiful home. A raging river of mud had carried the furniture all over the house smashing bookcases, tearing out doors, clogging appliances and cabinets. Everywhere, it was a scene of total devastation.

But there, in the middle of the living room, stood the armoire, upright. Remembering my beloved photograph, I reached up to check for it. To my amazement it was just as I'd left it: untouched, perfectly dry and completely safe. It was proof that God hears my prayers. In the difficult days ahead— and even now—I cherished this demonstration of God's love. It's how I knew, in the face of terrible suffering, that God had a plan for my life.

This is the only picture I have of my dear grandmother, Ella D. Smith. She did not know how to read or write, so I have no recipes in her handwriting; I learned her recipes by working with her side-by-side. As this photo shows, Grandmama had an inborn understanding of quality, taste and style. Her elegance inspired me to reach for the stars. When I was a young woman, she told me, "Linda, when you don't have a dime to your name, put on your best dress, and your high heels, hang your purse on your arm and hold your head high. You can always be proud of who you are."

When I started my business in Georgia— GG's Fine Foods, LLC---a wonderful friend of mine by the name of Janice took this picture,  *and many other beautiful images of my specialty foods that we've used on the website and in marketing my products. Oh, if Grandmama could see me now!*

Chicken and Sausage Gumbo

Roux:
½ cup of all purpose cooking oil (a little more if needed, but not too much!)
1 Tablespoon of bacon drippings
1 cup flour (plain)

2 bay leaves, whole
1 large onion, chopped
2 cloves garlic, minced
1 cup of parsley, chopped fine
1 cup of celery, chopped
1 bell pepper, chopped
1 cup of green onions, chopped
1 gallon of water
4 chicken breasts, washed, cut up and seasoned with a little salt and pepper
1 pound of smoked sausage or Andouille, hot or mild (optional)

Tips:

A Roux is the paste that forms the soup base. It's what gives this dish a deep, rich flavor.

If you want tomatoes, add ½ cup. The smoked sausage or Andouille adds extra flavor.

Mix oil, bacon drippings and flour in a heavy pot over medium heat.
Stir constantly until roux is a dark brown. Add onion, garlic, parsley, celery, bell pepper and green onions. Reduce heat; you don't want it to burn. Add water. Bring to boil and add chicken, sausage and bay leaves. Reduce heat and let simmer until chicken is done.
Serve over cooked rice.

GG's Gumbo

Jambalaya Ya Ya!

2 Tablespoons vegetable oil
1 large onion, chopped
1 large bell pepper, chopped
1 clove garlic, minced
1 cup celery, chopped fine
2 cups raw long grain white rice (parboiled works best)
½ pound chopped ham
1 pound smoked pork sausage, sliced
1 bay leaf
Salt to taste
GG's Bodacious Creole Seasoning® to taste
3 Tablespoons chili powder
3 Tablespoons paprika
¼ teaspoon thyme
¼ teaspoon cumin
3 Tablespoons tomato paste
1 cup diced peeled tomatoes

In a large pot or deep skillet, heat oil.
Add onion, bell pepper, garlic and celery.
Sauté on medium heat until tender. Add rice with amount of water according to package directions. Add remaining ingredients. Reduce heat and let simmer until rice is tender. If water boils out and rice is not cooked, add more hot water, a little at a time.

To complete the Ya Ya!, you can add a seasoned chopped grilled chicken breast and ½ cup whole kernel corn.
For extra flavor, you can add more Thyme and Cumin.
You can always add hot sauce or Cayenne for a more bodacious flavor! It's up to you to make it spicy or mild. It's your dish!

Jambalaya Ya Ya

Mama's Old Fashioned Hamburgers

2 pounds ground beef (chuck is preferred)
1 cup onion, chopped
1 teaspoon salt
1 teaspoon pepper
1 egg
3 Tablespoons vegetable oil

Mix the ground beef, onions, salt, pepper, and egg very well.

Put a handful of meat in your hand and roll into a ball.
Slowly flatten and shape into a patty.
Place a small amount of vegetable oil in a skillet, along with the patty. Cook on medium heat until cooked the way you like it.

Tip: Honey, dress the burger up on a toasted bun or bread with mayonnaise, ketchup, a little yellow mustard, lettuce and tomato and serve a pickle on the side. The ultimate taste comes from fixing a burger dressed the way you like it.

Oyster Po-Boy

16 ounces of vegetable oil
½ cup of yellow fine corn meal
Salt and pepper to taste
10 large oysters, raw
2 teaspoons butter, melted
6 inch French bread
8 dill pickle chips

Tip: It's great with an ice cold root beer, my favorite!

Preheat oil in pot or deep skillet.
Season meal with salt and pepper, then roll oysters in meal to coat all over.
Shake off excess meal.
Butter bread lightly, and toast until light brown.
Drop oysters into hot oil and cook until golden brown. Drain.
Place pickles and oysters on toasted bread, and top with a little of GG's Remoulade Sauce.

Poultry

I just love chicken. It's always good and versatile.
And it isn't a holiday without turkey!

Grandma's Old Fashioned Smothered Chicken

½ chicken cut up
Small bottle (16 ounces) of vegetable cooking oil
Salt & pepper to taste
Pinch of Cayenne pepper
2 cups of flour
2 medium onions, cut into rings
2 ½ cups of water

Wash chicken very well.
Pat dry with paper towel.
Heat cooking oil in a heavy skillet on medium heat.
Season chicken with salt, pepper, and Cayenne pepper.
Roll in flour and dust off excess flour.
Cook until golden brown, browning on both sides.
Place chicken on paper towel to drain any excess oil.
Pour out grease only leaving the flour crumbs in the bottom of the skillet.
Add about 2 teaspoons of flour to that and brown.
This will darken and thicken gravy.
Place onions into the drippings.
Stir and place chicken back into the skillet.
Add water.
Place lid onto skillet and cook on medium heat until tender. If any oil settles on top of chicken, just skim it off.
Check the taste for more spices.
Serve over rice!

Mama's Chicken in a Cream Gravy

1 whole chicken, cut up
2 quarts water
2 cups of onion, chopped
Salt and pepper to taste
½ cup flour

First wash the chicken good.
In a heavy pot, add chicken, water and onions.
Add salt and pepper to taste.
Cook on medium heat until the chicken is almost done.
Take your flour, put it in a cup with a little water and mix until it becomes soupy, then add to chicken.
It will look white at first but it is going to cream as it thickens.
Pick out the lumps of flour, if any.
Serve over rice.

Ella Dees' Fried Chicken

1 whole fryer cut up
Salt and pepper to taste
Vegetable oil, enough to deep fry; this could take 32
ounce or more, enough to fully submerge the pieces
of chicken
4 cups flour
Pinch of cayenne, if you want it spicy add a little
more

Cut up and wash chicken. Drain and pat dry.
Add salt, pepper to taste, and refrigerate for 2 hours.
Prepare flour with salt and pepper.
Heat oil. You test your oil by sprinkling a little flour
in it; if the flour fries, it's ready.
If you have a turkey bag add flour and put in 4 pieces
of chicken at a time, shake it up.
If you don't have a turkey bag, a brown paper bag
will work just fine.
Shake excess flour from the chicken before adding to
the grease.
When the chicken floats to the top, it's done.

Deep Fried Cajun Turkey

12 - 14 pound turkey
Salt and pepper to taste
3 Tablespoons GG's Bodacious Creole Seasoning®
½ teaspoon liquid crab boil
1 teaspoon paprika
2 teaspoons garlic, granulated
2 teaspoons onion, granulated
5 gallons peanut oil

Wash turkey thoroughly and rub down with all spices. If possible, refrigerate overnight. Submerge the turkey into peanut oil at about 300 degrees and cook for 45 minutes to one hour depending on the size of the turkey. Cook until the internal temperature is 165-170 degrees for the breast or 175-180 degrees for the thigh.

A small turkey takes approximately 45 minutes at 300 degrees.
A large turkey takes approximately 1 hour at 300 degrees.

Tip:
Don't try this recipe without the proper equipment. You will need a large deep-fryer; it's best to do the frying outdoors, and have a fire extinguisher nearby.

After frying:
Let the turkey rest on paper towels for 15 minutes before slicing.

Oven Baked Turkey

7 – 9 pound turkey
GG's Bodacious Creole Seasoning® to taste
Salt and pepper to taste
2 cups onion, chopped
2 cups celery, chopped
2 cups bell pepper
½ stick butter
1 Turkey bag (follow bag instructions)

Wash turkey and lightly sprinkle with GG's
Bodacious Creole Seasoning® all over, inside and
under the turkey.
Salt and pepper to taste.
Put about 1 cup of onion, 1 cup of celery, and 1 cup
of bell pepper in the cavity of the turkey.
Put the rest in the bag under the turkey.
Add butter.
Turkey makes its own juice so you don't have to add
water.
Bake at 325 degrees for approximately 3 to 3 ½
hours, but make sure to refer to package directions.

Every day is a day of Thanksgiving

Holiday time
was a family affair at
our house. Thanksgiving was my favorite.
My mother and grandmother would be up
cooking all night long. Our dinner consisted of
turkey, dressing, potato salad, peas, green
beans, sweet potatoes, ham, cranberry sauce,
fruit salad, coconut cake; pound cake drizzled
with icing and that outrageous sweet potato pie.
I remember assisting my grandmother and
asking her to show me how to do this and that.
On Thanksgiving Day, the house would be full
of family and friends. The great aromas of these
fine foods would fill the house and the love
would wrap around you like a
warm blanket on a
winter's night.

A Word about Ingredients...

ALWAYS use the best quality ingredients you can find—it makes all the difference in the world. To get old-fashioned flavors, you have to use old-fashioned food--pure and natural. Farmstead dairy products and organic vegetables taste better because they're made the old-fashioned way, with care.

I also have to mention my love for Louisiana seafood! There's nothing like the distinctive flavor of our oysters, shrimp, crawfish, and the many varieties of fish we enjoy. Fishing is the life and legacy of New Orleans cuisine. If you buy Louisiana seafood, you know you're getting the best.

Pork, Beef & Game

Good meat is the centerpiece to a good meal. It's not that hard to make a great main dish—you can do it!

Barbeque Ribs

Hat's off to my Uncle J.D. for teaching me his secrets to cookin' up a good barbeque! Thanks Uncle J.D.—you the man!

1 slab of ribs, pork or beef
Salt and pepper to taste
1 large onion, chopped
2 cloves garlic, minced
Water (enough to cover ribs in pot)
Barbeque sauce

Tip: Beef ribs take longer to cook but before you remove the meat, make sure it's tender.

Wash the ribs well, cut off all the excess fat. (If pork ribs, cut every two ribs. For beef, cut every rib.) Season meat and sprinkle with onion and garlic. Put in a pan, cover, and refrigerate overnight. In a large pot, place ribs, onions & garlic with enough water to cover them entirely.
Cook on medium heat. Add water when needed, just a little at a time. You don't want to lose the flavor.
Cook until tender, then drain.
Place in a pan and add barbeque sauce, any flavor you want or sprinkle with a dry rub.
Bake at 350 degrees until sauce begins to bubble, or about 15-20 minutes with a dry rub.

Pork Roast with Sweet Glaze Topping

2 pound pork roast, lean
½ teaspoon granulated onion
Salt and pepper to taste
Pinch of cayenne
1 ½ cups water
½ cup onions, chopped
1 teaspoon butter

Tip: You can add a swig of Bourbon to the glaze for a more robust flavor.

Glaze:

1/3 cup light brown sugar
1 cup pineapple juice (use a can of chunk pineapple, reserve the juice)
2 Tablespoons soy sauce
½ teaspoon flour
A little pinch of cayenne
Combine ingredients and bring to medium boil.
Add half can pineapple chunks.

Wash roast. Season, add onions and butter and refrigerate overnight. When ready to cook place roast in pan with 1 ½ cups water. Cover with foil and bake on 350 degrees for approximately 1 hour and 15 minutes or until tender. Make glaze while roast is in oven. Remove from oven when tender.
Saturate with glaze and return to oven for 20 minutes without foil on top.

This glaze is sweet with a kick!

Food Made to Order	Nothing Good Happens Fast

Slam Ham

6-5 pound boneless ham
6 slices of pineapple
6 cherries

Ham Glaze:
½ cup pineapple juice
½ cup light brown sugar
1/3 cup of honey
1 Tablespoon prepared mustard
1 teaspoon apple cider vinegar
½ teaspoon allspice
1/8 teaspoon cloves
1 teaspoon cornstarch

In a pot or deep skillet, mix all ingredients for glaze.
Over medium heat, cook until it thickens, then
remove from heat.
Place the ham in a pan or casserole dish lined with
foil.
Brush on glaze. I mean saturate it.
Then arrange pineapples and cherries on ham, using
toothpicks to secure.
Place in a preheated oven at 350 degrees for about an
hour and 15 minutes.

Stuffed Bell Peppers

4 medium to large bell peppers
Water (2 inches in pot)
1 ½ pound ground beef (get ground chuck if possible)
1 Tablespoon vegetable oil
1 large onion, finely chopped
2 green onions, chopped
2 stalks celery, chopped
2 Tablespoons fresh parsley, chopped
1 clove garlic, minced
Salt and pepper to taste
1 egg, beaten
¼ cup milk
½ cup seasoned bread crumbs, plus a little extra for topping

Cut off and throw away the tips of the bell peppers. Cut in half and remove seeds and the membrane. Rinse.

In a heavy pot or saucepan, add about 2 inches of water with a pinch of salt. Place peppers upright in pot. Bring water to a boil and cook for about 5 minutes. Remove peppers and drain. Set aside.

Filling:
Cook the ground meat in the vegetable oil. Drain. Add onions, green onions, celery, parsley, garlic and some salt and pepper. Cook until brown, then let it cool down. Add the egg, milk and the bread crumbs.

Mix, then stuff the bell peppers. Dress them up by sprinkling a little more of the bread crumbs on top. Bake uncovered in a preheated 350 degrees oven for 30 minutes or until lightly brown.

People are eating every day, but they are starving for the things that matter most—love, family and fellowship. Bring your family back to the dinner table. Slow down, and eat your food.

Auntie Janie's Roast Ooh La La
(Crock Pot Roast)

1 - 2 pound beef Chuck roast
Salt & pepper to taste, plus a sprinkle of meat tenderizer
1 teaspoon GG's Bodacious Creole Seasoning®
1 cup vegetable oil
½ cup flour
1 onion, sliced
1 clove garlic, minced
1 cup water
2 white Russet potatoes cut in chunks
1 bag frozen mixed vegetables

Wash roast. Leave whole or can cut against the grain to desired thickness.
Sprinkle with salt, pepper, meat tenderizer, and Creole seasoning.
Heat the vegetable oil in a skillet on medium heat.
Dust the roast with flour then shake off the excess.
Place the roast in the skillet and brown on both sides.
Remove the roast from the skillet and place on paper towels to soak away the grease. Place the onions in the bottom of the crock pot then add the meat.
Add one cup water, potatoes, and frozen vegetables in that order.
Cook for approximately 3 - 4 hours on low heat, or until tender.
Serve over rice.

Spaghetti and Meatballs

1 ½ pounds ground meat
1 egg, beaten
½ cup seasoned bread crumbs
2 cloves garlic, minced
2 Tablespoons parsley
1 cup onion, chopped fine
Oregano to taste
2 Tablespoons evaporated milk
8 ounce can tomato paste
8 ounce can tomato sauce
½ cup diced fresh tomatoes
4 cups water, or more to thin to desired consistency
Salt and pepper to taste
1 package spaghetti, cooked according to package
directions (I prefer thin.)

Mix meat, egg, breadcrumbs, ½ garlic, ½ parsley, ½
onion, oregano, and evaporated milk.
Form into meatballs. Bake in a 350 degree oven until
browned and cooked through, about 25 – 35 minutes.
Remove from pan and drain.

To make the sauce, place the remaining garlic, onion
and parsley in a pot with the tomato paste and tomato
sauce. "Fry" for a few minutes stirring constantly.
Slowly add the water and bring to a boil.

Reduce the heat to low and simmer adding water as
needed for the desired thickness. Add oregano to

taste. Add the meatballs to the sauce 10-15 minutes before serving.
Serve over spaghetti.
Sprinkle with parmesan cheese if desired. Fresh parmesan is fantastic.

Great with garlic bread!

Tip: For a more robust flavor, do half ground meat and half ground pork.
For a lighter version, use ground turkey.

Smothered Liver and Onions

1 pound calf liver
Salt and pepper to taste
½ cup flour
2 large onions, cut into rings
½ stick of butter

You will need a large heavy skillet.
Season liver with a little salt and pepper, then dip in flour until covered on both sides.
Put a couple of tablespoons of butter into the skillet on medium heat.
Add liver and brown on both sides. If you need a little more butter, it's ok.
Remove quickly.
Add onions on bottom and sauté.
Add liver and the rest of the onions.

This is great with grits!

Tip: The key to tender liver is not cooking it long. The longer it cooks, the tougher it gets.

Aunt Mary's Venison (Deer)

Venison neck bones
1 bell pepper, chopped
1 onion, chopped
1 teaspoons GG's Bodacious Creole Seasoning®
1 Tablespoon black pepper
1 clove garlic, minced
Salt and pepper to taste
Water

Gravy:
1 Tablespoon vegetable oil
2 ounces flour
1 cup water

Make sure the necks are cut into neck bones.
Clean and wash them. Put in a pot with enough water
to cover meat. Add all the ingredients.

For gravy, mix oil and flour
and cook on low heat stirring
continuously until dark
brown. Add water slowly
while stirring.
Pour the gravy over the meat
and seasoning mixture.
Cook on medium heat until
completely tender, 2 to 3
hours or until the meat falls
off the bone.
Serve over rice.

Tip: Remember, the size of the neck depends on the size of the deer. You might have to add more seasoning.

Seafood & Fish

Louisiana is known for its seafood. For real, authentic Creole flavors, buy Louisiana seafood. If it's not available in your area, look for the freshest fish and shellfish you can find.

GG's Seafood Omelet

3 eggs
Cayenne pepper to taste
Pinch of granulated garlic
1 teaspoon olive oil
1 Tablespoon diced onion
6 shrimp (medium size)
¼ cup portabella mushroom
(optional)
Pinch of salt and pepper
Butter flavored non-stick spray
1 Tablespoon cheddar cheese
1 Tablespoon mozzarella cheese

You need a spatula, skillet, bowl and butter flavored nonstick spray.

Topper:
3 Tablespoons salsa
1 Tablespoon sour cream
½ Tablespoon cheddar cheese
½ Tablespoon mozzarella cheese

First crack the eggs and put them in the bowl Add cayenne and garlic and whip with a fork about a minute. Preheat skillet on medium heat. Add olive oil, onions, shrimp, mushrooms, salt, and pepper. Sauté. When shrimp turn lightly pink, they are ready. Remove from skillet and make sure the skillet is still smooth. Spray pan once with non-stick spray then add eggs. Cook on medium heat. The minute the eggs begin to bubble add shrimp and cheese and fold over, flip, then remove. Place on a pretty plate and add topper.

GG's BBQ Shrimp

1 cup salted butter
½ Tablespoon vegetable oil
1 Tablespoon paprika
½ teaspoon cayenne
1 teaspoon basil
1 teaspoon oregano
6 bay leaves (whole)
3 teaspoons minced garlic
2 teaspoons lemon juice (fresh)
Salt and pepper to taste
2 ½ pounds of fresh whole shrimp (keep the shell on)

Get a heavy saucepan or skillet.
Put in the butter then the oil and melt together on medium heat. Add all the other ingredients except for the shrimp (you don't want them to over cook). Stir your sauce; you don't want it to stick.
As soon as it begins to boil turn down the heat, let simmer for about 10 minutes then add your shrimp and turn the heat up to medium.
When the shrimp turn pink that is a good sign they are ready.

These are great with French bread for dipping or served over grits.

I Tried It and I Like It!

Creole Smothered Okra and Tomatoes with Shrimp

Okra
Vegetable oil
Onion
Fresh ripe tomatoes
Salt and pepper to taste
Shrimp
Smoked sausage, cooked and drained (optional)

The amount of each ingredient is not given for this recipe. Use more or less of each ingredient to suit your taste.

Sauté okra in vegetable oil until no longer slimy.
Add onions, tomatoes, salt, and pepper.
Smother (partially cover) the pot and cook until the okra is tender adding water as needed.
Add the shrimp and sausage once the okra is tender and smother for an additional few minutes until the shrimp turn pink.

Listen Love, this dish is great with baked chicken or fried chicken and cornbread.

Quick Fish Dish

1 teaspoon granulated onions
1 teaspoon granulated garlic
2 teaspoons steak sauce (brown, such as A-1 Sauce)
A little water
3 teaspoons olive oil
3 pieces of filet catfish

Combine onion, garlic, steak sauce, and water in a
mixing bowl.
Brush over and under fish.
Heat your skillet on medium heat; add olive oil,
place fish into skillet and cook on both sides until
done, approximately 10-15 minutes.
Keep checking and turning fish over, don't let it
stick.
This will work on top of the stove or in the oven.

*Tip: Great with a
green veggie and rice
pilaf. Great with
tilapia too.*

Fried Catfish

2 pounds of catfish filets
Salt and pepper to taste
2 cups yellow cornmeal (plain and finely ground)
Pinch of cayenne
Lemon wedges for garnish and to squeeze onto fish
if desired
Enough vegetable cooking oil to fill ½ the pot
(A Dutch oven or heavy pot is best)

Wash for catfish: (optional)
1 egg beaten
2 Tablespoons water

Rinse catfish and pat dry with paper towel.
Season with a little salt and pepper.
Also season your cornmeal with cayenne and a little
salt and pepper to taste.
The wash is optional—if you use it, dip the fish in
the wash, then in the breading; or if you want, just
dip the fish into the cornmeal, roll around to cover
both sides.
Check your oil by putting a piece of meal into the oil
and if it fries, go on and fry fish, it's ready.

Salmon Croquettes

1 can of pink salmon, drained
1 egg beaten
½ cup onion, chopped fine
1 teaspoon baking powder
Salt and pepper to taste
1 ½ cup vegetable oil
¼ cup flour
A little flour for dusting just before going into the skillet.

Drain salmon well. Beat an egg; set aside.
In a mixing bowl, add remaining ingredients and mix well. Add beaten egg and stir. Sprinkle ¼ cup flour into mixture and stir. Form into small patties, not too thick. You want them to have a little depth. Dust the patties lightly with flour, and then fry until golden brown.

Tuna Casserole

1 pound package fettuccini noodles
Pinch of salt
1 teaspoon cooking oil (your choice)
2 cans cream of celery soup
2 cans of tuna, packed in water; drain and reserve ½
cup of the liquid
Salt and pepper to taste

Cook fettuccini according to package directions or
until al dente, adding a pinch of salt and the oil.
Drain fettuccini and set aside.
Put the two cans of soup into a mixing bowl.
Add ½ can of water, or use juice from tuna.
Add salt and pepper to taste.
In a casserole dish, layer noodles, tuna, and soup.
Repeat until all gone but save a little soup for the top.
Preheat oven to 350 degrees.
Bake until the first bubble appears, then remove from
oven and serve.

Tip: If you want it super good, layer top with your favorite cheese.
Serve with sweet peas and garlic bread on the side!

Side Dishes

Side dishes can be so good, you'll want to make a meal out of them! Save the leftovers and pack 'em for lunch the next day.

Old Fashioned Grits

4 cups water
½ teaspoon salt
1 ½ cups old-fashioned grits
1 teaspoon bacon grease

In a medium saucepot bring water to a boil then add salt and grits. Grits will pop so be careful; turn down the burner and boil on medium heat. Cook until grits start to thicken; add the bacon grease. Keep stirring so they don't stick.
Add hot water as needed. Cook until creamy, about 20 to 40 minutes.

Tip: The key to cooking grits is to boil the water before adding the salt. Once the salted water is rolling, add the grits.

Never throw away the leftovers! Use leftover grits to make Cheesy Grits Casserole—so good as a side dish, or even for breakfast.

Cheesy Grits Casserole

4 cups water
½ teaspoon salt
1 ½ cups of old-fashioned grits
1 ½ cup cheddar cheese
1 egg beaten
1/3 cup milk
1 teaspoon butter

In a medium saucepan bring water to a boil.
Add salt and grits.
Cook 20 to 40 minutes, until done.
Mix cheese (save a little for topping), egg, milk and butter together then add to grits and stir well.
Butter a small-medium casserole dish, add mixture, and sprinkle remaining cheese on top.
Bake at 350 degrees for about 15 minutes.
A good indication that they are ready is when the cheese on top is melted.

The same recipe works for garlic grits, just add garlic cheese or one clove of minced garlic.

Passing It On...

Greens

This recipe works for Mustard Greens, Collards, Turnips, Cabbage or Kale:

Always wash the greens. And I mean wash 'em!

If you are going to use meat, you don't need a pot full of meat to give it flavor, just a little bit.
If you are weight-watching, you can use turkey bacon. It works!

Mustard greens: if you are going with fresh, you have to pick and clean them.
Wash them thoroughly and cut them up in medium pieces.

3 Tablespoons canola oil
6 strips of bacon
½ small onion, chopped
Salt and pepper to taste.

First heat your oil over low heat, and then add bacon and onion. Bacon may pop so be careful.
When bacon starts curling, add greens and a little water because greens make their own water if fresh.
If frozen, add 1 ½ cups of water. Cook until tender.
Salt and pepper to taste.

Yams/Sweet Potatoes

4 large sweet potatoes
1 cup sugar
2 Tablespoons light brown sugar
4 Tablespoons butter
Pinch of salt
1½ cup water
1 Tablespoon vanilla

Peel potatoes.
You can cut like French fries or slice like chips.
Put them into a large pot. Add sugars, butter, salt,
water and vanilla. Stir occasionally to avoid sticking.
Put on low heat with the lid on and cook until tender;
test with a fork and when the fork inserts easily, the
potatoes are done. Transfer to a serving dish and
enjoy!

Lets Cook Green Beans

½ onion, chopped
4 cups fresh green beans, snapped or cut into 1"
pieces
1 Russet or Yukon potato, diced into small pieces
Dash of salt
Pinch of pepper
2 Tablespoons butter
2 cups water

Honey, I wash everything. Wash the green beans
first. They cook better when you cut them, or snap
them in pieces.

Heat butter in skillet on low heat.
Add the onions and keep stirring until they soften.
Add green beans, potatoes, salt, pepper and water.
Tilt lid on skillet, don't cover completely.
Cook on low heat until the green beans and potatoes
are tender—about 20 to 30 minutes.
You can add seasoning to your taste.

Now remember to stir your green beans gently and
tilt your lid so they don't stick.
If you need a little more water, add it.

Granny's Macaroni and Cheese

½ pound elbow macaroni
1 cup evaporated milk
1 egg, beaten
1 ½ cups whole (sweet) milk
Salt and pepper to taste
1 teaspoon GG's Bodacious Creole Seasoning®
1 Tablespoon butter (NOT margarine!)
2 cups cheddar cheese
½ cup cheddar cheese for topping

Make the macaroni following the package
instructions and drain well.
Mix all of the ingredients, except for the cheese for
topping.
Pour into a casserole dish greased with butter.
Top with cheese and bake at 350 degrees until the
top is brown and bubbling.

Tip: If you want to fancy it up some, use a three-cheese blend for topping.

Spicy Corn

4 ears of corn
4 cups water
1 Tablespoon liquid crab boil
Pinch of salt
1 lemon cut in half
2 celery stalks, cut in pieces
½ onion, cut in half
1 bay leaf

Wash corn.
Place in pot.
Add water, enough to cover corn, crab boil, salt,
lemon, celery, onion and bay leaf.
Bring to a boil, and cook until it's tender, about 10 to
15 minutes.

It's good all by itself, or buttered.

Tip: You can throw in a few new potatoes or a quartered Russet potato.
Keep the skins on!

Squash Casserole

3 medium to large yellow squash
1 medium to large onion, chopped
3 Tablespoons butter
Salt to taste
GG's Bodacious Creole Seasoning® to taste
½ teaspoon cayenne pepper
1 Tablespoon sugar
1 hunk of cornbread or about 2 large handfuls
(leftovers are great)
1 egg, beaten
1 ½ cup grated cheddar cheese

I wash everything y'all. Wash the squash and cut into slices. Cut onion. First, put butter in skillet on low heat. Let it melt. Add onions. Stir until onions caramelize. (To caramelize, cook until the onions are clear and very brown from cooking in their own juices). Add squash.

Cover and stir occasionally. The squash will make its own juices. Add salt, Creole seasoning, cayenne pepper, and sugar. When it has cooked down, taste and add more seasoning if desired.

Then take that hunk of cornbread and crumble it in a separate bowl. Add the egg to the corn bread and stir it up. Let the squash mix cool a bit then add to the cornbread mix.

Put everything in a greased casserole dish and bake at 350 degrees for 15 minutes. Remove from the oven, sprinkle with cheese. Return to the oven and bake until the cheese is melted.

Make plenty. They will want seconds. Thank you Lord! Finally, a Squash Casserole that's good!

Simply Smothered Potatoes

6 Russet potatoes
1 medium onion
¼ cup of vegetable cooking oil
½ clove of garlic, minced
Salt & pepper to taste
¼ cup of water

Peel potatoes, wash and cut like medium potato chips.
Peel onion and cut into rings.
Heat oil in a heavy skillet on medium heat.
When oil is hot enough, add onions and garlic.
Cook until softened, and then add potatoes, salt, pepper and water.
Tilt lid and cook on medium heat until tender.
Stir occasionally so that potatoes do not stick.

My Favorite Foods

Fried Green Tomatoes, Fried Okra, Fried Eggplant

Honey, we dippin' & fryin'!

3-4 medium green tomatoes cut ¼ inch thick
or
2 pounds okra, cut into ¾ inch pieces
or
1 large egg plant, peeled and sliced

Salt and pepper to taste
1 cup white corn meal
1 cup flour
Pinch of cayenne (optional)
2 eggs, beaten
Oil for frying

Tip: Eggplant is excellent rolled in seasoned breadcrumbs!

GG's Remoulade Sauce goes great with anything fried

Season (tomatoes, okra, or eggplant) with salt and pepper.
Mix cornmeal and flour.
Season with cayenne and a little salt and pepper.
Dip into the egg, then roll around in cornmeal and flour mixture.
Deep fry in enough hot oil to cover.
Fry until golden brown.

Real Red Beans and Rice

1 pound dried red kidney beans
8-10 cups water
1 cup celery, chopped
1 cup onion, chopped
1 clove garlic, minced
2 Tablespoons fresh parsley
chopped
4 large bay leaves
Salt to taste
½ pound of ham or pickled meat
or 1 pound smoked sausage sliced
(a ham bone will work too)

Tip: This recipe will work for any kind of dry bean. Most places refer to red beans as kidney beans but in New Orleans, Darlin', we call them Red Beans. Make sure the beans are light red. Darker beans tend to be a little tougher.

Sort your beans and rinse well.
Put them in a heavy pot and add
water.

You cannot make good red beans in a non-stick or light-weight pot!

Bring to a boil and add all of your ingredients, except
meat.

If you have a ham bone, put it in at this point,
otherwise wait an hour or so, then add ham, pickled
meat, or sausage. If you use pickled meat, cook first
to boil some of the salt out. Pour off water and add
meat to the beans.

Watch your food. Beans take a lot of water and you don't want it to cook out. Add more water as needed. Reduce the heat, and the beans should cream. If they don't, smash a few against the pot and they will.

Red Beans & Rice

෨෨

I remember a
time or two
when things
were rough for
my mom, and
we ate this
simple meal by
candlelight,
because the
electricity was
off: it consisted
of cooked rice,
with a little
butter and a
sprinkle of sugar
over it. I'll cook
that right today,
because it helps
me feel grateful.

෨෨

Dessert

One of my favorite memories was watching my grandmother whip up a cake by hand, and anxiously awaiting the bowl and the spoon—to lick the batter! If you don't bake a cake from scratch, how are the kids going to lick the bowl? That's reason enough to whip up a cake.

Aunt Mary's Bodacious Three-Layer Cake
(This works with any kind of icing)

3 cups of flour (plain)
2 ½ teaspoons baking powder
3 sticks of butter
3 cups of sugar
5 eggs
1 cup milk (add a little more if needed)
1 teaspoon pure vanilla extract

Preheat oven to 350 degrees.
Sift flour and baking powder together and set aside.
Cream butter until it gets a little fluffy then add sugar and continue to cream
for 5 minutes.
Add eggs one at a time and beat well after each egg.
Alternate adding flour and milk.
Add vanilla.

Tip: Eggs, butter, and milk work better at room temperature.

Use three 9 inch pans
Grease with butter, add flour, and shake the pan until it is covered. Knock off excess flour.
Divide the cake batter evenly into the pans.
Bake for 35 minutes until brown around the edges.
To tell when cake is done, stick a fork or toothpick in the center, and if it comes out clean it's done.

Aunt Mary's Bodacious 3-Layer Cake

Pineapple Filling *(optional)*

1 can crushed pineapple (reserve juice)
2 Tablespoons sugar
1 teaspoon flour (can add more if needed)
1 teaspoon pure vanilla extract (or any flavor you want)

Tip: You can substitute any filling for your cake, even ice cream.

In pot on medium heat combine pineapple juice, sugar, flour and vanilla.
Stir, then add crushed pineapple.
Remove from heat and cool.
Divide filling and spread evenly between cake layers.
Ice cake and you are ready to serve!

German Chocolate Upside-Down Cake

1 cup coconut (I add just a little extra)
1 cup chopped pecans (I add just a little extra)
1 box German chocolate cake mix, prepared according to package instructions
1 stick butter
1 - 8 ounce package cream cheese
1 box confectioner's sugar

In a 13" x 9" greased pan, sprinkle the coconut and pecan pieces on the bottom.
Mix cake mix according to the package directions.
Pour cake mix over coconut and pecans.
In a saucepan, add the stick of butter and cream cheese.
Melt that down enough then add the confectioner's sugar and mix until smooth.
Pour cream cheese mixture on top of cake mix.
Place in oven on 350 degrees for about 35-45 minutes.

Let cool to room temperature, then flip upside down on a platter.

This recipe is very rich!

Smash Pound Cake

3 cups sugar
2 sticks real butter at room temperature
6 eggs at room temperature
3 cups of plain flour
½ pint of whipping cream
¼ teaspoon pure almond extract

Cream sugar and butter until smooth.
Add eggs, one at a time.
This is important because you must make sure
everything is mixed well.
Add flour one cup at a time.
Put a little whipping cream in as you mix.
Add almond extract.
Pour batter into a Bundt pan greased with melted
butter and dusted with flour.
Put cake in the center of a cold oven, and set the
oven for 325 degrees.
Bake 1 hour and 15 minutes or until done.
Always check with a toothpick. If it comes out clean,
it's done.

Icing

This icing can be used for cakes, cookies, brownies, etc.

3 cups confectioner's sugar
½ cup milk
1/3 cup butter, melted
1 Tablespoon pure vanilla extract (or any flavor you like)
1 Tablespoon evaporated milk
¼ teaspoon cream of tartar (optional)

Combine ingredients into a bowl and mix.

Makes enough for a 2-layer cake.

Tips: You can use coconut milk for a more bodacious flavor!

Sweet Potato Pie

4 large sweet potatoes
1 teaspoon fresh lemon juice
1/3 cup brown sugar
1/3 cup white sugar
1/4 teaspoon cinnamon
1/4 teaspoon allspice, ground
1/4 teaspoon nutmeg
½ teaspoon salt
½ teaspoon pure vanilla extract
¼ cup evaporated milk
1 large egg, beaten
1 pie shell, 9 inch, unbaked

Peel sweet potatoes. Cut into big chunks.
Put into a heavy pot.
Add enough water to cover them completely.
Boil on medium heat until they become tender. Drain
and remove potatoes to a bowl to cool.
Once cooled, add the other ingredients, except the
egg, and mix well.
Add the eggs when you know that the potatoes will
not cook them—potatoes must be completely cool.
Mix everything well.
Pour mixture in the pie shell.
Preheat oven to 350 degrees.
Cook pie for 35 to 45 minutes.
When a knife stuck in the middle comes out clean,
the pie is done.

Lemon Ice Box Pie

Tip: You can use a graham cracker crust instead of vanilla wafers.

Filling:

1 can of condensed milk
6 egg yolks (reserve whites for later)
6-7 lemons (fresh squeezed without seeds)
1 Tablespoon pure vanilla extract
Vanilla wafers (half package)

Meringue:

6 egg whites
12 Tablespoon sugar

In a bowl, add condensed milk, 6 egg yolks and beat. Add lemon juice and vanilla. Your filling should be thick.

Prepare a crust by layering vanilla wafers on the bottom of a pie dish. Add filling mixture. Layer, alternating with vanilla wafers and filling till there is nothing left. Put into refrigerator while you prepare meringue.

For meringue topping, whip egg whites with electric mixer until fluffy. Add sugar 2 tablespoons at a time, whipping until the mixture stands in peaks. Remove pie from refrigerator and spread meringue on top. Bake in a 425 degree oven for about 5-10 minutes or until meringue is brown. Chill completely and serve.

Banana Pudding

2 ½ cups whole milk (I call this sweet milk)
1/3 cup flour
3 egg yolks (reserve egg whites for meringue)
1/2 Tablespoon pure vanilla extract
½ teaspoon lemon juice
¾ cup sugar
4 - 5 bananas
½ package vanilla wafers

Filling:
Mix milk, flour, egg yolks, vanilla extract, lemon
juice, sugar and cinnamon into a double boiler.
If you do not have one, make your own by using a
pot with water and a smaller pot or a heat proof bowl
on top. Stir until mixture thickens, then remove from
heat.

Prepare a crust by layering vanilla wafers on the
bottom of a pie dish. Add sliced bananas and then
filling . Layer with vanilla wafers, bananas and
filling till there is nothing left.
Put into refrigerator while
preparing meringue.

Meringue:
3 egg whites
6 Tablespoon sugar

For meringue topping, whip
egg whites with electric mixer

Tip: You can use a graham cracker crust instead of vanilla wafers. You can also use whipped cream instead of meringue.

until fluffy. Add sugar 2 tablespoons at a time, whipping until the mixture stands in peaks. Remove pie from refrigerator and spread meringue on top. Bake in a 425 degree oven for about 5-10 minutes or until meringue is brown.

Making Banana Pudding

Custard Cups

1 cup sugar
¼ teaspoon cinnamon
¼ teaspoon nutmeg
1 Tablespoon pure vanilla extract
½ teaspoon pure almond extract
2 cups whole milk
1/8 teaspoon salt
2 whole eggs
3 egg yolks

In a mixing bowl, mix all ingredients except for milk. Mix well.
In a small pot, bring milk to a medium boil. Turn off.
Slowly add milk to the ingredients in the bowl, stirring as you add.
Pour in oven safe custard cups.
Fill a baking pan with about 2 inches of water, and set the custard cups in the pan to make a water bath.
Bake in a preheated oven at 325 degrees for about 45 minutes or until done.
When custard cups begin to brown, you can sprinkle brown sugar on the tops. The sugar will caramelize.
When you stick a toothpick in the middle and it comes out clean, it's ready.
Let cool and refrigerate.
Serve cold.

Warm Peaches with Vanilla Ice Cream

2 Tablespoons salted butter
4 to 5 large ripe peaches (peel and slice
approximately ½ inch thick)
2 Tablespoons brandy (optional, but why not?)
1 teaspoon nutmeg
1 teaspoon cinnamon
¼ teaspoon allspice
1/8 teaspoon cloves
1 teaspoon pure vanilla
extract
3 Tablespoons sugar
(taste for sweetness)
Just a little bit of water
Vanilla ice cream

Tip: This same method will work with almost any fruit.

In a saucepan, add butter on low heat.
When melted added peaches, sauté.
Add all other ingredients, except the ice cream.
Add a small amount of water.
Cook until the peaches are very tender.

Serve warm with ice cream on the top.

Peach Cobbler

I call it Cobbler because I use a spoon to scoop it out and serve.

3 cup of peeled and sliced peaches
1 stick butter
1 ½ cups sugar
¼ cup of brown sugar
1/2 teaspoon cinnamon
1/2 teaspoon nutmeg
2 teaspoons flour
2 pie crusts (unbaked)

For topping:
1 Tablespoon melted butter
½ teaspoon sugar

Tip: If you don't have the time to make the crust, buy two ready-made piecrusts. They work just as well—and it makes cobbler so easy to put together.

Honey, get your pot and put in all ingredients, except the crust and topping ingredients. Cook until it thickens on medium heat, and then remove.

Put filling into one of the pie shells. With a fork, prick the bottom of the other pie shell several times. Then, using a sharp knife, cut out the bottom and place the round on top of the pie. Brush with melted butter and sprinkle with the sugar.

Bake at 350 until golden brown.

Daisy Bells Blackberry Cobbler

Scoop it up with a big spoon!

1 ½ cups sugar
1 stick butter
2 ½ cups blackberries
1 Tablespoon pure vanilla extract
1 teaspoon nutmeg
2 teaspoons flour
2 nine inch pie crusts, uncooked

Put all ingredients, except pie crust, into a pot.
Cook on medium heat until it begins to thicken.
Keep stirring because you do not want it to stick.
Once it thickens, remove from the heat.

Put filling into one of the pie shells. With a fork,
prick the bottom of the other pie shell several times.
Then, using a sharp knife, cut out the bottom and
place the round on top of the pie. Brush with melted
butter and sprinkle with the sugar.

Bake at 350 until golden brown.

Tea Cakes

3 cups flour (plain)
¼ teaspoon salt
¼ teaspoon baking soda
1 teaspoon baking powder
¼ teaspoon cream of tartar
(optional)
1 Tablespoon butter, melted
2 cups sugar
2 eggs
1/3 cup whole milk
3 Tablespoons buttermilk
½ Tablespoon pure vanilla extract
1/2 teaspoon pure almond extract

You can sprinkle a little sugar on them or wait until they bake, then drizzle with a light icing, or sprinkle with powered sugar-any will do. These go great with tea or coffee!

First sift dry ingredients together into a bowl. Set aside. In another bowl, cream butter and sugar.
Then add eggs, whole milk, buttermilk, vanilla and almond extracts to the butter and sugar.
In a third bowl, mix dry ingredients alternately with wet ingredients. This should form a dough.
Chill dough for a couple of hours.
Grease your cookie sheet with butter or nonstick spray.
Pinch off dough and roll into 2 inch balls for a thick cookie or flatten for a thinner cookie.
Leave a space in between so cookies don't touch and have room to spread while baking.

Bake at 400 degrees for approximately 10 - 12 minutes or until edges are brown and crispy-then the cookies are done. They will be softer in the middle.

Tea Cakes

ଓଓଗ୍ଧ

My grandmother used to store tea cakes in an old syrup can, because it was airtight and kept them fresh. Every time we went to her house, we looked for the can. The tea cakes were always so good and fresh!

113

The Proof is in the Pudding!

Crème de Menthe Brownies

Brownies:
½ cup butter
1 cup sugar
4 eggs, beaten
1 cup all-purpose flour
½ teaspoon salt (optional)
1 teaspoon pure vanilla extract
1 can chocolate syrup (16 ounce)

Cream butter and sugar. Add eggs and other ingredients in order given. Blend well and pour into greased 13" x 9" pan. Bake at 350 degrees for 20-25 minutes. Let cool in pan while preparing the other layers.

Middle layer:
2 cups powdered sugar
½ cup butter
2 Tablespoons crème de menthe
Mix and spread over cooled brownie. Leave in pan.

Glaze:
1 cup chocolate chips
6 Tablespoons butter
Melt chocolate chips and butter in a double boiler, stirring constantly. When completely smooth, top the crème de menthe layer with glaze. Cool completely. Cut and serve. For a festive touch, add crushed candy canes on top!

Classic Creole Pralines

1 ½ cup sugar
1 ½ cup light brown sugar
½ teaspoon salt
1 cup of milk
½ stick salted butter
1 teaspoon vanilla extract (pure)
1 teaspoon lemon extract (pure)
2 ½ cups pecan pieces

Mix sugars, salt and milk.
Stir over low heat until the sugar dissolves.
Cook to 238 degrees on a candy thermometer.
Cool to 220 degrees.
Add butter, both extracts and pecans.
Beat with a spatula until creamy.
While mixture is still soft, drop by spoonfuls onto a
piece of buttered wax paper, leaving space in-
between.
Let them cool and harden.

Honey, they are ready to eat!

Lost Bread

1 cup milk
½ teaspoon cinnamon
½ teaspoon nutmeg
1 Tablespoon pure vanilla extract
½ cup heavy whipping cream
1 cup brown sugar
1 stick melted butter
1/8 teaspoon ginger
3 eggs
3 inch piece French bread sliced diagonally or 4 pieces of sliced bread
Confectioner's sugar and cinnamon for dusting

In a bowl, mix all the ingredients except the bread.
Grease the skillet with butter, put on low heat.
Then dip bread into mixture.
Place 2 pieces of bread into the skillet and turn heat up to medium high.
Watch carefully, keep lifting bread until golden brown, and turn over to heat the other side.
When finished sprinkle with a little cinnamon and confectioners sugar.

Serve with a hot cup of coffee.

Beverages

There's nothing that says hospitality like a tall, refreshing glass of homemade lemonade, or a hot cup of coffee. It only takes a little extra care to make a drink extra-special.

Ice Cold Lemonade

12 large lemons
1 gallon of cold water
3 cups sugar
½ teaspoon pure lemon
extract

Roll the lemons until soft.
Cut in half and squeeze out
juice.
Add to water.
Add sugar and lemon
extract.
Stir very well until sugar is
dissolved.
Refrigerate until ice cold.

Tip: Don't put the rind in the lemonade; it will make the lemonade bitter. Only use the rind for garnish. Lemonade may be used as a base drink for ice tea.

Lemonade looks pretty served in a frosted glass with
a fresh lemon wedge or a sprig of mint.

It's Tea, Simple but Delicious

12 teabags
1 gallon water
1- 1/2 cups sugar
2 lemons (optional)

Boil tea bags in a gallon of water.
Add sugar and continue cooking for 5 minutes.
Turn off heat and remove tea bags with a slotted spoon.
Let cool.
Add 1 quart of water then place in the refrigerator.
Add sliced lemons (optional).
Serve in a tall glass over ice with lemon wedges for garnish.

Mocktail

Champagne glasses
Sugar
Honey
Crushed ice
100 % cranberry juice cocktail
Sweet lemonade made with real lemons
Lemon and cherries for garnish

Put a little bit of sugar into a small bowl.
Smear honey around rim of champagne glass and dip glass into sugar to frost the rim.
Add a little crushed ice to glass, ½ cranberry juice and half lemonade.
Garnish with a lemon (slice/wedge) and a cherry.

It is beautiful and very refreshing.

Talktails

To an 8 ounce glass full of crushed ice, add:
3 ounces champagne
3 ounces orange juice
Garnish with a slice of fresh orange with the rind on.

Put a limit on the Talktails, 'cause when you hear
"Child, let me tell you…"
…you know something juicy is coming!

3 Step Punch

2 liters of your favorite soda or ginger ale, ice cold
½ gallon of ice cream or sherbet
6 cherries

In a punch bowl add ice cold soda.
Place ice cream or sherbet in the middle.

As the ice cream or sherbet begins to melt, the punch
is ready to serve.

Tip: Throw in some cherries or your favorite fruit.

Real New Orleans Café Au Lait
(That's coffee to me!)

3 cups whole milk
1/2 cup heavy cream
8 cups of coffee with chicory (brewed and hot)
Sugar

Mix the milk and cream in a pan.
Slowly bring to a boil then quickly remove the pan from the heat.
Pour equal amounts of coffee and cream and mix into each cup.
The coffee is very important: make it strong.
Add sugar to taste.

Tip: Café au lait can be served ice cold as well. Just refrigerate and serve over ice using a half coffee and half milk mixture. It is great topped with whipped cream when served cold.

Café au Lait

Mama, Grandma---Don't TELL me
that recipe---Write it down!

About the Author

Linda "GG" Gibson

Linda "GG" Gibson lives with her three children—Demetra, Latanya and Regshawn in Roswell, Georgia. When she is not in the kitchen or running operations at GG's Fine Foods and GG's Grab & Go, she enjoys entertaining, listening to live jazz & blues, and dancing. GG brings her enduring love for New Orleans culture and food to her new community in Georgia, leading to many new friendships. For the Love of Gumbo, Let's Cook! is GG's first cookbook.

Index

A

B

H

I

J, K, L

M, N